Alligators
and Other Crocodilians

Concept and Product Development: Editorial Options, Inc.
Series Designer: Karen Donica
Book Author: Gari D. Fairweather

For information on other World Book
products, visit us at our Web site at
http://www.worldbook.com

For information on sales to schools and libraries
in the United States, call 1-800-975-3250.

For information on sales to schools and libraries
in Canada, call 1-800-837-5365.

World Book, Inc.
233 N. Michigan Ave.
Chicago, IL 60601

Library of Congress Cataloging-in-Publication Data

Alligators and other crocodilians.
        p. cm. -- (World Book's animals of the world)
    ISBN 0-7166-1218-6 -- ISBN 0-7166-1211-9 (set)
     1. Alligators--Juvenile literature. 2. Crocodilians--Juvenile literature. [1. Alligators.
    2. Crocodilians.] I. World Book, Inc. II. Series.

    QL666.C925 A6 2001
    597.98--dc21

                                                    2001017527

Printed in Singapore
1 2 3 4 5 6 7 8 9 05 04 03 02 01

Animals of the World

Alligators
and Other Crocodilians

When do I feel like high walking?

World Book, Inc.

Contents

What Is a Crocodilian? 6

Where in the World Do Crocodilians Live? 8

What Is Home to American Alligators? 10

Why Do Alligators Seem So Lazy? 12

Do Alligators Breathe Underwater? 14

How Do Alligators Move on Land? 16

What Do Alligators Eat? 18

Why Are Alligators Such Good Hunters? 20

How Do Alligators Communicate? 22

Are Alligators Good Parents? 24

Who's That Chirping from the Nest? 26

Do American Alligators Have Enemies? 28

How Many Kinds of Alligators Are There? 30

What Are Caimans? 32

Why Are Black Caimans So Unusual? 34

Do you want to see me gallop?

Why do I stick so close to Mom?

Which Caiman Likes the Rain Forest? 36

Which Is the Smallest Crocodilian? 38

How Do You Tell an Alligator from a Crocodile? 40

Do Any Crocodiles Live in North America? 42

What Do Crocodiles Do in the Dry Season? 44

Which Crocodiles Set Traps? 46

Do Crocodiles Share Their Food? 48

Why Are Mugger Parents So Unusual? 50

Which Crocodiles Are at Home in the Sea? 52

Which Crocodile Runs the Fastest? 54

Who Are These Creepy Crocodilians? 56

What Is a False Gavial? 58

Are Crocodilians in Danger? 60

Crocodilian Fun Facts 62

Glossary 63

Index 64

Why do people call me "Saltie"?

What Is a Crocodilian?

A crocodilian *(KRAHK uh DIHL ee uhn)* is
a reptile that has rough, scaly skin and thick,
bony plates along its back and tail. Alligators
are crocodilians. So are crocodiles, caimans
(KAY muhnz), and gavials *(GAY vee uhlz)*.

Like other reptiles, crocodilians lay eggs and
breathe air through lungs. They are also cold-
blooded. Their body temperatures change with
the air and water temperatures around them.
They lie in the sun to warm up, and they swim
to cool off.

When you look at a crocodilian, you may think
you are looking at a dinosaur. In a way, you are.
Crocodilians have been around for millions of years.
In fact, they are the only surviving members of the
archosaurs *(AHR kuh sawrz)*, the dinosaurs known
as the ruling reptiles.

American alligator

Where in the World Do Crocodilians Live?

Crocodilians are somewhat picky about where they live. Their habitats need to have the right climate. And they need to be near water.

Most crocodilians live near the equator, in tropical parts of the world. Here, the climate is warm or hot all year around—just right for cold-blooded reptiles. Of the 23 species of crocodilians, only 2 live in cooler climates. They are the American alligator and the Chinese alligator.

The habitats of crocodilians include swamps, lakes, streams, and rivers. Crocodilians spend part of their time in the water and part of their time on land.

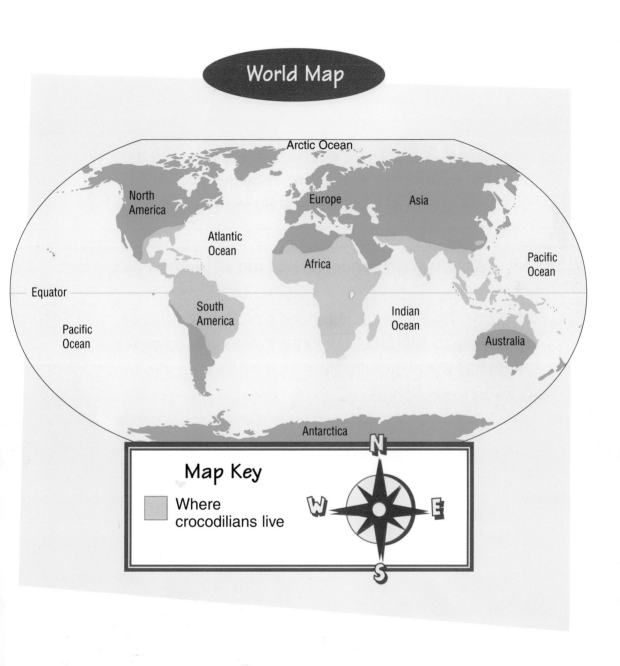

World Map

Arctic Ocean

North America

Europe

Asia

Atlantic Ocean

Africa

Pacific Ocean

Equator

Pacific Ocean

South America

Indian Ocean

Australia

Antarctica

Map Key

Where crocodilians live

N

W

E

S

9

What Is Home to American Alligators?

American alligators live in watery areas of the southeastern United States. They live in lakes, ponds, and marshes. They live in rivers, creeks, and swamps. They even live in canals.

Alligators often dig burrows to live in. They use their mouths and clawed feet to rip and dig the earth. They sweep away loose mud and dirt with their tails. A burrow might be a hole or a tunnel in a mud bank. It might be a 'gator hole dug into the bottom of a pond.

'Gator holes are an important part of a swamp. Mud and plants pushed aside by the alligator become rich soil where new, healthy plants grow. During a drought, or dry period, a 'gator hole still holds water. It is home to both the alligator and its young. Fish, birds, and other animals live in and near the 'gator hole, too. They may stay until the rains return. But sometimes, the guests become dinner!

'Gator hole

Why Do Alligators Seem So Lazy?

Alligators spend a lot of time doing nothing—both in and out of the water. But they are not lazy! By doing nothing, alligators control their body temperatures.

Since alligators are cold-blooded, they often lie in the sun to warm up. This is called basking. To keep from getting too hot, an alligator gapes, or lies with its mouth open. An alligator gapes for the same reason a dog pants—to let heat escape from its body.

A crocodilian's heart has four chambers. These chambers help control an alligator's temperature. If an alligator begins to overheat, more blood flows near the surface of the skin. The warm blood gives off its heat to the cooler surroundings.

Of course, an alligator can always move into the shade or cool water to beat too much heat!

American alligator

Do Alligators Breathe Underwater?

Alligators can't breathe underwater. But they can stay there for an hour or more. When an alligator submerges, or goes underwater, its heart slows down. The alligator doesn't have to breathe as often, but the heart still pumps blood to important organs, such as the brain.

Like many animals, alligators have two eyelids to protect each eye. But when an alligator submerges, a third eyelid covers each eye. This eyelid is clear. The clear eyelids act like swim goggles.

Flaps of skin cover an alligator's ears at all times. But when an alligator submerges, special flaps close off its nostrils and the back of its throat. Nostril flaps keep the alligator from breathing in water. The throat flap lets an alligator open its mouth to catch prey without swallowing water.

Alligators are excellent swimmers. But they don't swim with their legs. They swim by sweeping their tails from side to side.

American alligator

How Do Alligators Move on Land?

Alligators move three different ways on land. They high walk, belly walk, and belly run.

Alligators high walk when they aren't in a hurry. In a high walk, an alligator's body is up off the ground. Look at the alligator in the picture. Its legs are under the body, holding it up. The alligator walks like a mammal, one leg at a time. Alligators move slowly when they high walk. But they can high walk for long distances.

When an alligator belly walks, it moves like a lizard. It twists from side to side and pushes the earth with its legs and feet. Alligators belly walk to cross muddy ground or to slide quickly into water.

To escape danger, alligators sometimes belly run. This is just a faster belly walk, with the alligator's belly off the ground. Alligators can belly run only for short distances.

American alligator

What Do Alligators Eat?

Alligators eat many different animals. They eat fish, frogs, snakes, and crabs. They eat turtles, birds, and small mammals. Large alligators also eat pigs, deer, and cattle. Alligators can eat just about any animal that lives in or comes near the water!

Inside an alligator's strong jaws are up to 80 sharp, cone-shaped teeth. An alligator uses its jaws and teeth to catch prey. With one snap, a large alligator can crush through bones or a turtle shell. But the alligator cannot chew its food. It must swallow its prey whole or tear it into pieces.

An alligator goes through thousands of teeth in a lifetime. Alligators often lose teeth tearing prey. But that's okay for a young alligator. When one falls out, a new tooth grows in its place. Older alligators don't regrow as many teeth as young ones do.

American alligator

Why Are Alligators Such Good Hunters?

Alligators are good hunters because they are so patient. They do not waste energy chasing their meals. They usually wait for food to come to them.

An alligator uses its senses of smell, hearing, and sight to find prey. Then it submerges and swims in for the attack. The alligator strikes so quickly that the prey is caught by surprise.

An alligator strikes in different ways. It may lunge onto the shore to grab an animal. It may leap 5 feet (1.5 meters) into the air to grab birds above. It may sweep its head sideways to grab fish and turtles swimming by.

Alligators don't use up a lot of energy, so they eat less often than other animals do. Inactive alligators may even go several months without eating!

American alligator

How Do Alligators Communicate?

Alligators communicate in many ways. They use body language to send signals. They also use sound and touch.

When alligators use body language, they send signals with their bodies. These signals may be warnings. A large alligator raises its head and slaps its jaw against the water, as if to say "Watch out! I'm stronger than you." A small alligator submerges to say "Okay, you're the boss!"

During courtship, alligators also use sound and touch. Both males and females bellow and growl. They rub necks and noses. The male slaps his jaw on the water and blows water bubbles to impress the female. He may do a water dance by shaking his body very quickly. This makes the water jump and "dance" along the alligator's back. The shaking also makes a sound so low that humans can't hear it. But the female alligator can. And it seems to impress her a lot!

Alligator doing a
water dance

Are Alligators Good Parents?

Alligators are some of the best parents in the reptile world. Mothers guard their nests and help the eggs hatch. And sometimes both parents look after and protect the young.

A female alligator builds a nest on the ground. She uses her mouth to gather plants. She uses her feet and tail to push the plants and soil into a large mound, or pile, about 3 feet (0.9 meter) high and 7 feet (2.1 meters) wide. Then she lays her eggs in a hollow at the top of the mound nest and covers them up.

Alligators do not warm their eggs by sitting on them. They let the nest warm the eggs. As plants in the nest decay, they give off heat. This warms the eggs.

Even though a mother alligator does not sit on her eggs, she is always nearby. She guards the nest to keep away egg-eating animals, other alligators, and people.

American alligator
with nest

Who's That Chirping from the Nest?

About nine weeks after a female alligator lays her eggs, chirping sounds come from the nest. The babies are hatching! But are they males or females? That depends on the temperature of the nest. If a nest stays warm, males hatch. If a nest is cool, females hatch. If the temperature is in-between, both males and females hatch.

When a mother alligator hears chirps, she uncovers the eggs. She picks up the hatchlings with her mouth and carries them to the water. She will also roll any unhatched eggs in her mouth to crack the shells and help the babies hatch.

Hatchlings are about 9 inches (23 centimeters) long. They can swim and catch their own food right away. But they still need protection, so they stay close to their mother. A hatchling may even bask on its mother's head or back. If a hatchling is in danger, it cries out. This brings the mother right away. Hatchlings may stay with their mothers for a year or more.

American alligator
with hatchlings

Do American Alligators Have Enemies?

Alligators are very large animals. A full-grown male may be more than 12 feet (3.7 meters) long. Animals as big as this have very few enemies. In fact, adult alligators fear only other adult alligators and people. Young alligators, however, have many enemies.

Dangers begin for young alligators even before they hatch. For example, animals such as raccoons and skunks steal and eat the eggs of American alligators. They wait for the mother to leave the nest to swim or to feed. Then they quickly raid the nest.

A hatchling like the one you see here faces many dangers. Foxes, bears, snakes, and birds of prey may snatch up hatchlings for a tasty meal. Young alligators may even have to watch out for larger alligators!

American alligator
hatchling

How Many Kinds of Alligators Are There?

There are only two kinds of alligators. These are the American alligator and the Chinese alligator. A Chinese alligator is about half the size of an American alligator.

Much of what we know about alligators comes from studying American alligators. Chinese alligators are very shy, so little is known about their habits. We do know that they eat snails, mussels, fish, and small mammals. We also know that Chinese alligators spend a lot of time in their burrows.

Both American and Chinese alligators can survive colder temperatures than other crocodilians. When a pond freezes over, an American alligator may survive the cold by lying in shallow water and poking its nostrils through a hole in the ice. A Chinese alligator, however, usually enters its burrow to escape from the cold. During this time, the alligator is dormant, or inactive. It doesn't eat. It may stay in its burrow for months.

Chinese alligator

What Are Caimans?

Caimans are alligators that live in Central and South America. They are usually smaller than American alligators. Most caimans (also spelled *caymans)* have bony ridges between their eyes.

The most widespread caiman is the common caiman. It is often called the spectacled caiman because of its bony ridge. The ridge makes the caiman look as if it has spectacles, or eyeglasses.

Like alligators, common caimans live in many different water habitats. They make their homes in swamps, large rivers, lakes, and flooded grasslands. Common caimans also live in human-made habitats, such as canals and cattle ponds.

Spectacled caiman

Why Are Black Caimans So Unusual?

Black caimans are the largest caimans. They can grow to be as large as American alligators. But what makes them unusual is that they don't lose their "baby stripes."

Most crocodilian hatchlings have markings that help them blend into their surroundings. American alligator hatchlings have yellow stripes to help them hide in grasses along the shore. These stripes fade over time. But the markings on black caimans do not fade.

Black caiman hatchlings have gray heads and black bodies that are marked with rows of white dots. As the hatchlings grow, their gray heads turn brown. But their stripes and dots never fade away entirely.

Black caiman

Which Caiman Likes the Rain Forest?

The Schneider's *(SCHNY duhrz)* dwarf caiman lives in the dense rain forest of South America. It spends much of its time on the forest floor. The streams in its habitat are shallow and rocky. The water may not even cover this caiman.

Schneider's dwarf caimans are small. Males grow to a length of only 5 1/2 feet (1.7 meters). Like other crocodilians, these caimans have many sharp scutes, or scales, that stick out. But their scutes are sharper than most. Dwarf caimans also have bony tails that are stiffer than other crocodilian tails. This extra body armor helps protect the caimans from the sharp rocks found in the rain forest streams.

Schneider's dwarf caimans rarely bask. Instead, they spend much of the day lying in hollow logs or under fallen leaves. They sometimes build their nests beside termite mounds. The heat from the termite mounds helps warm the nest.

Schneider's dwarf caiman

Which Is the Smallest Crocodilian?

The smallest crocodilian of them all is Cuvier's *(KYOO vee ayz)* dwarf caiman. When it is an adult, it is less than 5 feet (1.5 meters) in length. Like the Schneider's dwarf caiman, it avoids open areas. But it also avoids the dense forest. Cuvier's dwarf caimans prefer flooded areas near forests. And they are often found in swift-flowing waters or near waterfalls.

Cuvier's dwarf caimans are heavily armored. They have thick bony plates along their backs and sides. They also have short snouts and high, smooth foreheads. They are the only crocodilians to have sloping foreheads. These small caimans spend much of the day in their burrows.

Cuvier's dwarf caiman

How Do You Tell an Alligator from a Crocodile?

The easiest way is to look at the animals' heads. Alligators and caimans have wide, U-shaped snouts. Crocodiles have narrow, V-shaped snouts. But there are other differences, too.

The upper jaws of alligators and caimans are wider than their lower jaws. When the mouth is closed, the teeth in the lower jaw are covered. A crocodile's upper and lower jaws are nearly the same size. When its mouth is closed, some teeth in the lower jaw are still seen.

Alligators and caimans usually live in fresh water. Crocodiles are found in fresh water *and* in salt water. Crocodiles have salt glands on their tongues. Extra salt from food or water leaves the crocodile's body through these salt glands.

Finally, alligators and caimans are shy and will usually avoid humans. Many crocodiles are bold. They are less likely to avoid humans.

Comparison of Crocodilians

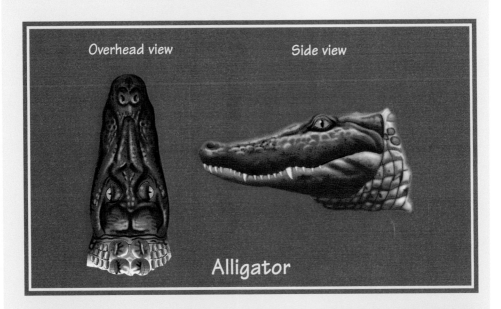

Overhead view   Side view

Alligator

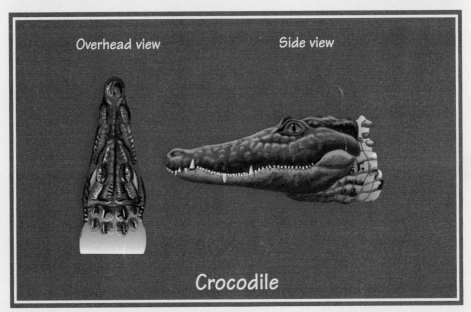

Overhead view   Side view

Crocodile

Do Any Crocodiles Live in North America?

Yes, one kind of crocodile does live in North America. American crocodiles live on islands in the Caribbean *(kar uh BEE uhn)* and along the coast of Central America. Some also live in the southernmost part of Florida.

American crocodiles can grow to be very large, as large as 20 feet (6.1 meters). But most of these crocodiles are smaller than American alligators.

American crocodiles spend their days resting in sheltered waters, among thick plants, or in their dens. They come out at night to feed. They build nests by digging holes in the sand or in a riverbank. Sometimes, if there is no place to dig, American crocodiles build mound nests.

American crocodile

What Do Crocodiles Do in the Dry Season?

In tropical areas, seasons can be rainy or dry. During the dry season, many crocodilians must search for places that still have water.

The Orinoco *(ohr uh NOH koh)* crocodiles of South America are one example. During the rainy season, their grassland homes are flooded. Rivers flow in places that are dry at other times of the year. There are many places to swim, bask, and feed. But in the dry season, many of these areas dry up. The crocodiles must return to their watery burrows or search for new watery pools.

Orinoco crocodiles are very protective parents. At night, hatchlings may wander off by themselves to look for food. But during the day, their mother stays with them in a group called a pod. She protects them for a good reason. In South America, giant otters prey on young crocodiles. These otters can reach lengths of 7 feet (2 meters).

Orinoco crocodile

Which Crocodiles Set Traps?

Crocodilians have many different ways to catch prey. Nile crocodiles of Africa even set traps to catch fish.

A good time to watch trap-setting is when great numbers of fish are found in one area. This happens when fish are searching for food. It also happens when fish swim upstream to spawn, or lay eggs.

Nile crocodiles use their bodies to set traps. They line up next to each other in a stream. As fish swim by, the crocodiles catch them with a snap of their jaws. A single crocodile may also use its body to block a part of a stream. This forces fish to swim around the crocodile and—snap! The crocodile swings its head sideways and grabs the fish.

Nile crocodile

Do Crocodiles Share Their Food?

Crocodiles do seem to share food, but probably not out of kindness. The real reason they share is out of need. Often, crocodiles need other crocodiles to help them eat prey that can't be swallowed whole.

The Nile crocodile eats fish. But it also preys on large animals such as zebras and wildebeests *(WIHL duh BEESTS)*. Once a crocodile sights its prey, it submerges and swims in close for the attack. Then it grabs the animal, drags it into the water, and drowns it. The noise and splashing of the kill attracts other crocodiles.

Even though one crocodile does the killing, several crocodiles help eat the prey. The crocodiles take turns biting, twisting, turning, and rolling to tear off bite-sized pieces. After a few bites, a crocodile may swim away. Another crocodile takes its place. Larger, more dominant crocodiles usually get most of the food.

Nile crocodiles with wildebeest

Which Crocodiles Are at Home in the Sea?

Many crocodiles can live in fresh water and in salt water. But Australian saltwater crocodiles spend more time in salt water than any other crocodile. Salties, as they are called, can even swim hundreds of miles to reach new territories. Some spend so much time at sea that they have barnacles, a kind of sea animal, growing on them!

Australian saltwater crocodiles are the largest reptiles in the world. They can reach lengths of 23 feet (7 meters). Still, these giant crocodiles can leap high out of the water. When this happens, it looks as if they are walking on their tails!

Salties are very territorial, and they will attack to defend their territories from other crocodiles. Salties also have attacked and killed humans. This makes the Australian saltwater crocodile one of the most feared crocodilians.

Australian saltwater
crocodile

Which Crocodile Runs the Fastest?

Two kinds of crocodiles live on the continent of Australia. And both hold crocodilian records. The Australian saltwater crocodile is the largest. The Johnston's crocodile, or Australian freshwater crocodile, is the fastest.

Johnston's crocodiles are small and shy. They avoid humans and run if they feel threatened. Sometimes a run turns into a bounding gallop. First, the back legs push the animal forward. Then the front legs hold it up while the back legs swing forward for another push. Johnston's crocodiles can gallop as fast as 10 miles (16 kilometers) an hour.

Johnston's crocodiles live in freshwater lakes, streams, and swamps. These small crocodiles have long, narrow snouts and very sharp teeth—perfect for catching and eating fish.

Johnston's crocodile

Who Are These Creepy Crocodilians?

They are gavials, which are also known as gharials *(GAHR ee uhlz).* A gavial looks like a crocodile. But it has a very long and very narrow snout. This snout sets the gavial apart from other crocodilians. A male gavial has a round growth at the end of his nose that makes him look rather "creepy."

A gavial's narrow jaws are not strong enough to catch large animals. But they are designed to catch fish. A narrow snout can snap shut quickly. And sharp teeth easily hold onto wiggling, slippery fish.

Gavials live in river habitats in India. They spend almost all their time in the water. When they do come on land to bask or to nest, they cannot walk as other crocodilians do. They don't have the leg muscles needed to stand. So gavials must belly slide or swim wherever they want to go.

Gavials

What Is a False Gavial?

The animal you see here is called a false gavial. This crocodilian has a long, narrow snout. But little else is known about it. Scientists are not even sure if the false gavial is a member of the gavial family or the crocodile family.

False gavials live in freshwater habitats. They often swim in slow-moving waters that are thick with plants and other vegetation. And false gavials eat fish as well as small mammals.

Like many crocodilians, false gavials build mound nests. But they do not take care of their hatchlings. For this reason, very few false gavial hatchlings survive.

False gavial

Are Crocodilians in Danger?

Today, about 10 species of crocodilians are endangered, or in danger of becoming extinct. How did this happen? In the past, crocodilians were hunted for their hides, or skins.

To protect crocodilians, many countries passed laws to ban the hunting. These laws have helped many crocodilians, such as the Australian saltwater crocodile you see here. They also helped the American alligator. It was once endangered, but it was taken off the endangered species list in 1987.

Species such as the Chinese alligator, the black caiman, the Orinoco crocodile, the false gavial, and the gavial are still endangered. One reason is illegal hunting. Another is loss of habitat.

Today, conservationists are trying to help by setting aside land for crocodilians. Scientists also use incubators to hatch eggs so that more hatchlings can survive. The hatchlings are returned to the wild when they can take care of themselves.

Australian saltwater crocodile

Crocodilian Fun Facts

→ Some turtles lay eggs in alligator nests. Guarded by an alligator, the nest is a warm, safe place for turtle eggs.

→ An alligator's eyes have mirrorlike parts that reflect light. This helps the alligator see at night. It also helps people see it. A flashlight makes the alligator's eyes glow.

→ The oldest crocodile died in a Russian zoo in 1995. It was 115 years old!

→ Spanish explorers called the alligator *el lagar,* which means "the lizard."

→ A fossil found in Texas shows that alligators living at the time of the dinosaurs grew to be at least 30 feet (9 meters) long.

→ Some friends part by saying: "See you later, alligator!" or "In a while, crocodile!"

→ Alligator jaws have great crushing power. But the muscles that open them are so weak that a thick rubber band will keep the jaws closed.

Glossary

barnacle A hard-shelled marine animal that attaches itself to underwater surfaces.

bask To lie in the sun for warmth.

bellow The roar of a large animal.

burrow A hole or a tunnel dug for an animal's home.

climate The usual weather of a place.

cold-blooded Having a body temperature that changes with the surrounding temperature.

conservationist A person who works to save wildlife and natural resources.

courtship The act of finding and winning a mate.

den An animal's home.

dominant Ruling and most powerful.

dormant Not awake or active.

drought A long dry period.

endangered In danger of dying out.

extinct No longer existing.

gape To open the mouth wide.

'gator hole A hole in the bottom of a pond dug by an alligator.

habitat The area where an animal lives, such as a swamp.

hatchling An animal newly hatched from an egg.

hide The skin of an animal.

incubator A device that keeps eggs warm until they hatch.

mammal A warm-blooded animal that feeds its young on the mother's milk.

mussel A marine animal surrounded by two shells.

plate A flat, bony layer or scale.

pod A group of animals.

prey Any animal that is hunted for food by another animal.

reptile A cold-blooded animal with a backbone and scales.

scute A bony plate or scale that sticks out.

spawn To lay eggs and breed.

submerge To go under the water.

territory The place that animals keep for themselves.

Index

(**Boldface** indicates a photo, map, or illustration.)

Africa, 46
alligator, 6, 8, 10, 12, 14, 16, 18, 20, 22, 24, 26, 28, 30, 32, 34, 40, 42, 60
American alligator, **7**, 8, 10, **13**, **15**, **17**, **19**, **21**, **25**, **27**, 28, **29**, 30, 32, 34, 42, 60
American crocodile, 42, **43**
archosaur, 6
Australia, 54
Australian freshwater crocodile, 54
Australian saltwater crocodile, 52, 54, 60, **61**

back, 6, 38
basking, 12, 36, 44
black caiman, 34, **35**, 60
body, 34, 46
body temperature, 6, 12
breathing, 14

caiman, 6, 32, 34, 36, 38, 40, 60
Caribbean, 42
Central America, 32, 42
Chinese alligator, 8, 30, **31**, 60
climate, 8, 30
communication, 22
crocodile, 6, 40, 42, 44, 46, 48, 50, 52, 54, 56, 58, 60
crocodilian, 6, 8, 12, 30, 36, 38, 46, 50, 52, 56, 58, 60

Cuvier's dwarf caiman, 38, **39**
defense, 52
eggs, 6, 24, 26, 28, 50, 60
enemies, 24, 28, 44
extinction, 60
eyes, 14, 32
false gavial, 58, **59**, 60
feeding habits, 10, 14, 18, 20, 30, 42, 44, 46, 48, **49**, 54, 56, 58
feet, 10, 16, 24
Florida, 42
forehead, 38

'gator hole, 10, **11**
gavial, 6, 56, **57**, 58, 60
glands, 40
group, 44

habitat, 8, 10, 32, 36, 38, 40, 44, 52, 54, 56, 58, 60
hatchling, 26, 28, **29**, 34, 44, 50, 58, 60
head, 34, 40, 46
heart, 12, 14

India, 56

jaw, 18, 40, 56
Johnston's crocodile, 54

legs, 14, 16, 54
lungs, 6

mating, 22
mouth, 10, 24, 40, 50
movement, 16, 52, 54, 56
mugger, 50

nest, 24, **25**, 26, 28, 42, 50, 58
Nile crocodile, 46, **47**, 48, **49**
nostrils, 14, 30

Orinoco crocodile, 44, **45**, 60

plates, 6, 36, 38

scales, 36
Schneider's dwarf caiman, 36, **37**
size, 26, 28, 30, 32, 34, 36, 38, 40, 42, 52, 54
skin, 6, 12, 14, 34, 60
snout, 38, 40, 54, 56, 58
sounds, 26, 50
South America, 32, 44
spectacled caiman, 32, **33**
swimming habits, 14, 44, 52, 58

tail, 6, 10, 14, 24, 36
teeth, 18, 40, 54, 56
throat, 14
tongue, 40

United States, 10

world map, **9**

young, 10, 18, 24, 26, 28, 44, 50

Picture Acknowledgments: Front & Back Cover: © Fred Whitehead, Animals Animals; © Jean-Paul Ferrero, Auscape International; © Gerard Lacz, Animals Animals; © George McCarthy, Bruce Coleman Collection; © Roger De La Harpe, Animals Animals.

© Joyce & Frank Burek, Animals Animals 27; © Roger De La Harpe, Animals Animals 47; © Deeble & Stone /OSF from Animals Animals 49; © P. Evans, Bruce Coleman Collection 45; © Jean-Paul Ferrero, Auscape International 53; © Jeff Foott, Bruce Coleman Inc. 19; © David Hosking, Photo Researchers 11; © Jacques Jangoux, Photo Researchers 33; © Claudine Laabs, Photo Researchers 35; © Gerard Lacz, Animals Animals 57; © Jeffrey W. Lang 23, 55; © Jean-Marc LaRoque, Auscape International 5, 61; © Zig Leszczynski, Animals Animals 5, 29, 59; © George McCarthy, Bruce Coleman Collection 43; © Joe McDonald, Bruce Coleman Inc. 15, 39; © Wendell Metzen, Bruce Coleman Inc. 25; © David M. Schleser, Photo Researchers 37; © William Silliker, Jr., Animals Animals 13; © Therisa Stack, Tom Stack & Associates 7; © Lynn M. Stone, Bruce Coleman Inc. 31; © Grahame Webb, Wildlife Management International 4, 55; © Peter Weimann, Animals Animals 21; © Fred Whitehead, Animals Animals 3, 17.

Illustrations: WORLD BOOK illustration by Michael DiGiorgio 9, 41; WORLD BOOK illustration by Karen Donica 9, 62.

Crocodilian Classification

Scientists classify animals by placing them into groups. The animal kingdom is a group that contains all the world's animals. Phylum, class, order, and family are smaller groups. Each phylum contains many classes. A class contains orders, and a family contains individual species. Each species also has its own scientific name. Here is how the animals in this book fit in to this system.

Animals with backbones and their relatives (Phylum Chordata)

Reptiles (Class Reptilia)

Crocodilians (Order Crocodylia)

Alligators and caimans (Family Alligatoridae)

American alligator .... *Alligator mississippiensis*
Black caiman .... *Melanosuchus niger*
Chinese alligator .... *Alligator sinensis*
Cuvier's dwarf caiman .... *Paleosuchus palpebrosus*
Schneider's dwarf caiman .... *Paleosuchus trigonatus*
Spectacled (common) caiman .... *Caiman crocodilus*

Crocodiles and false gavial (Family Crocodylidae)

American crocodile .... *Crocodylus acutus*
Australian saltwater crocodile .... *Crocodylus porosus*
False gavial .... *Tomistoma schlegelii*
Johnston's (Australian freshwater) crocodile .... *Crocodylus johnsoni*
Mugger .... *Crocodylus palustris*
Nile crocodile .... *Crocodylus niloticus*
Orinoco crocodile .... *Crocodylus intermedius*

Gavial (Family Gavialidae)

Gavial .... *Gavialis gangeticus*